United States Regions

Southern Atlantic
Coast Region

Sue Vander Hook

Educational Media

rourkeeducationalmedia.com

Before Reading:

Building Academic Vocabulary and Background Knowledge

Before reading a book, it is important to tap into what your child or students already know about the topic. This will help them develop their vocabulary, increase their reading comprehension, and make connections across the curriculum.

1. *Look at the cover of the book. What will this book be about?*
2. *What do you already know about the topic?*
3. *Let's study the Table of Contents. What will you learn about in the book's chapters?*
4. *What would you like to learn about this topic? Do you think you might learn about it from this book? Why or why not?*
5. *Use a reading journal to write about your knowledge of this topic. Record what you already know about the topic and what you hope to learn about the topic.*
6. *Read the book.*
7. *In your reading journal, record what you learned about the topic and your response to the book.*
8. *After reading the book complete the activities below.*

Content Area Vocabulary
Read the list. What do these words mean?

abolitionists

coral reefs

diverse

dunes

economy

high tide

lumber

peninsula

plantations

tourism

tropical

After Reading:

Comprehension and Extension Activity

After reading the book, work on the following questions with your child or students in order to check their level of reading comprehension and content mastery.

1. *Explain what a tropical climate is. (Summarize)*
2. *Why is this region a popular vacation spot? (Asking questions)*
3. *What attracts people to the Atlantic Coast? (Text to self connection)*
4. *Why was slavery important in the South? (Summarize)*
5. *Why is farming a major industry in this region? (Infer)*

Extension Activity

Slavery was a large factor in the success of plantations in the Southern Atlantic Coast region. Many white businessmen felt slavery was needed in order to meet the demand of their crops. Others felt that slavery was wrong and that a human being should be treated equal regardless of the color of their skin. What do you think? Write an opinion piece to submit to your local newspaper. Explain why you are in favor of, or against slavery. Be sure to add examples to support your opinion.

Table of Contents

The Southern Atlantic Coast Region

Alligator

Have you ever seen an alligator? Have you touched a dolphin? Have you watched sea turtles lay eggs on a beach? Go to the Southern Atlantic Coast region of the United States. You will see them there.

The region is along the Atlantic Ocean. Miles of sandy beaches attract visitors. Warm ocean water is home to dolphins, sharks, and tuna. On land are rare plants, birds, and reptiles. The states in this region include Virginia, North Carolina, South Carolina, Georgia, and Florida.

Pelicans

Far to the south is Florida. It is a large **peninsula**. At the bottom is a chain of islands called the Florida Keys. The islands jut out 15 miles (24 kilometers) into the ocean.

Florida Keys

The city of Miami is on the Atlantic coast. It is a **diverse** city. More than half of Miami residents were born in another country. About 34 percent are Cuban. Others are from Africa, Nicaragua, Haiti, and Honduras.

Miles of flat beaches stretch along the Florida coast. The **tropical** climate makes Florida a great vacation spot. It is called the Sunshine State, although rain is plentiful during the summer months and the threat of a hurricane is always possible during hurricane season.

To the north are Georgia, South Carolina, and North Carolina. Many islands poke up out of the ocean. You might see a famous lighthouse.

The Cape Hatteras Lighthouse was completed in 1870. In 1999, it was moved back 2,900 feet (884 meters) from the eroding shoreline.

The coast has white sandy beaches. Sometimes the wind blows the sand and forms mounds called **dunes**. Salt water flows inland at **high tide**. It is called tidewater. Rivers and swamps twist through the land creating wetlands.

Many trees grow along the coast in coastal forests. Interesting plants and animals live there.

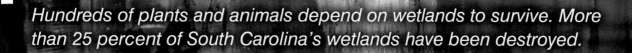

Hundreds of plants and animals depend on wetlands to survive. More than 25 percent of South Carolina's wetlands have been destroyed.

Sea Oats

Special plants grow on beaches and islands. Vines twist through the sand. Sea oats, a tall grass, grow in the sand. Vines and grass keep sand from eroding too much.

Further north is Virginia. The land is thick with grass and plants. It is a good place to watch for snakes and birds. You may see a raptor or snow geese. There are beavers, bears, and flying squirrels.

Many animals live in North and South Carolina. You may see whitetail deer or wild turkeys. In Florida there are panthers, alligators, and armadillos.

Armadillo

Florida Panther

Seagulls and pelicans fly over the Atlantic Ocean. Crabs crawl across the sandy beaches. Sea turtles lay their eggs there.

Grouper, snapper, and shrimp live in the ocean. Dolphins swim playfully, and manatees walk along the ocean bottom. Be careful of the dangerous spine of the stingray.

Huge fish like the ocean. The biggest are marlin, tuna, whales, and sharks. Sea trout and bass swim in rivers and bays.

Stingray

Most of the state of Florida is at sea level. This means the land is at the same level as the water.

Dolphins

Coastal History

Native Americans lived on the Southern Atlantic Coast. Then Spanish explorers came in 1513. Settlers from France and England arrived later. They settled large areas of land called colonies.

The English built Jamestown Colony in Virginia in 1607. They did not have enough food, and two years later, 80 percent of the colonists died. It was called "The Starving Time."

The colonies grew. Colonists planted tobacco, cotton, and rice, but they needed more workers in the fields. They purchased slaves from Africa. Slaves could not leave the **plantations**.

More than 200 years passed. People called **abolitionists** tried to end slavery. Farmers said their farms would fail without slaves.

Abolitionist
Harriet Tubman
1820–1913

The clash over slavery caused the Civil War. At the end of the war, slaves were freed.

Many people moved to the cities where there were tall buildings and new highways. Farming was not as important.

The first shots of the Civil War were fired at Fort Sumter in South Carolina.

Companies built hotels and amusement parks. The Southern Atlantic Coast became a good vacation spot. Visitors liked the warm climate.

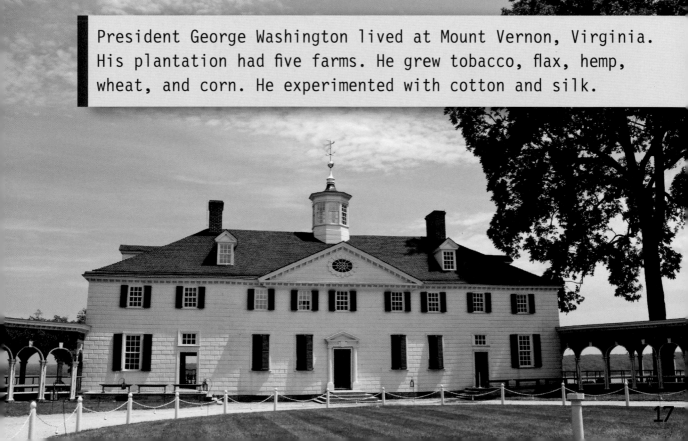

President George Washington lived at Mount Vernon, Virginia. His plantation had five farms. He grew tobacco, flax, hemp, wheat, and corn. He experimented with cotton and silk.

Business on the Atlantic Coast

What kind of jobs do Southern Atlantic Coast people have? In Florida, many people work in **tourism**. Their jobs are at hotels or amusement parks. Others are farmers. Florida grows 67 percent of all the oranges in the United States.

Disney World is a large amusement park in Orlando, Florida. Disney World has more visitors than any other amusement park in the world.

Fishing is an important industry all along the coast. Shrimp, lobsters, and crabs sell for high prices. In Virginia, oysters and crabs are especially popular. Atlantic coastal fishermen sell their fish all over the world.

Fishermen sell their catch to fish markets. Local shoppers buy fish from the fish markets.

Farming plays a large role in the **economy** of all the Atlantic Coast states. In Georgia, a person may work on a peanut or peach farm. Farming is also important in South Carolina. Farmers grow tobacco, cotton, and soybeans. Others cut down trees for **lumber**.

Tobacco or soybeans are popular crops in Virginia as well. Some farmers raise turkeys. Others grow grapes to make wine. Some people are coal miners.

Tobacco is an important crop for southern farmers.

The Atlantic Coast is where space shuttles were launched. The Kennedy Space Center on Cape Canaveral was built to launch them. All the Apollo manned flights to the Moon were launched there.

People of the Coast

What are people like on the Southern Atlantic Coast? They are friendly and polite. They welcome you into their homes. Family is very important. They are proud to be Southerners.

What do they wear? Some women wear large, colorful hats. They wear them with cool, flowing dresses. Men may wear sporty straw hats. Their suits are sometimes white with a bright tie.

For casual wear, people dress to stay cool. Shorts and tank tops are common.

For fun, people like water sports. They swim and surf in the ocean. Many go snorkeling or scuba diving. They see beautiful fish and **coral reefs** under the water.

Boating is a popular pastime. Some people water ski or parasail. Others fish, camp, or hike.

Southern Atlantic Coast people eat food special to the region. Some call it Southern food. For dinner, you may have fried chicken. On the side are biscuits or cornbread. Collard greens with bacon may be the

Mud Pie

vegetable. Dessert is mud pie. It is not made of mud, but with coffee ice cream and chocolate.

The South is known for grits. If you order eggs, they will often come with grits. For a drink, the sweet iced tea is not to be missed.

Food in Florida is interesting. You may be able to order alligator meat or try some conch soup. Conch meat is used for soups, salads, and burgers. The shell is used for decoration. If you blow into it, it makes a trumpet sound.

The Southern Atlantic Coast region is diverse. The food is interesting. The people are friendly. History is everywhere. The region provides many things to explore.

Blue crab is a favorite in South Carolina. They walk sideways on the beach. They dart about quickly in the water. Their strong claws can injure you. People catch them and cook them in boiling water. They make a special meal.

Southern Grits Recipe

Ingredients:

2 cups water

1-1/4 cups milk

1 teaspoon salt

1 cup quick cooking grits (not instant)

$\frac{1}{4}$ cup butter

Directions:

Put water, milk, and salt in a small pan. Bring to a boil. Slowly stir in the grits. Stir continuously until grits are well mixed. Return to a boil. Cover with a lid. Lower the temperature. Cook about 30 minutes. Stir occasionally. Add more water if necessary. Grits are done when they have a smooth texture.

Stir in the butter. Serve.

Places to Visit

- Crocodile Lake National Wildlife Refuge in Key Largo, Florida: Explore the protected land and water of Florida. Look for hundreds of interesting plants and animals.

- St. Augustine Alligator Farm Zoological Park in St. Augustine, Florida: See every species of crocodile, alligator, caiman, and gharial.

- Georgia Sea Turtle Center in Jekyll Island, Georgia: Watch sea turtles in their habitat. Watch them lay their eggs on the beach. Learn about Georgia's coastal ecosystem.

- Fort Sumter National Monument on Sullivan's Island, South Carolina: See where the American Civil War began on April 12, 1861.

- Cape Hatteras Lighthouse in Buxton, North Carolina: View the tallest lighthouse in the United States. Climb all 248 steps of the spiral staircase.

- Bodie Island Lighthouse in Nags Head, North Carolina: Climb a 156-foot (48 meter) lighthouse built in 1872. Look out over the Atlantic Ocean.

State Facts Sheet

Florida

Motto: In God We Trust.

Nickname: Sunshine State

Capital: Tallahassee

Known for: Beaches, Oranges,
Walt Disney World, NASA

Fun Fact: In Spanish, Florida means
"Feast of Flowers."

Georgia

Motto: Wisdom, Justice, and Moderation.

Nickname: The Peach State

Capital: Atlanta

Known for: Centennial Olympic Park,
Peaches

Fun Fact: Georgia is the official state
of the largemouth bass.

South Carolina

Motto: To Be, Rather Than to Seem.

Nickname: Palmetto State

Capital: Columbia

Known for: Myrtle Beach, Sea Turtles,
Tobacco

Fun Fact: The first battle of the Civil War
took place at Fort Sumter.

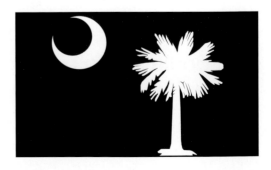

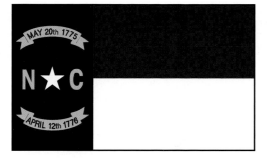

North Carolina

Motto: While I Breathe, I Hope Ready
  in Soul and Resource.

Nickname: Tar Heel State

Capital: Raleigh

Known for: Beaches, Wright Brothers

Fun Fact: The first English child
  born in America was Virginia Dare
  in Roanoke.

Virginia

Motto: Thus Always to Tyrants.

Nickname: The Old Dominion

Capital: Richmond

Known for: Tobacco, Jamestown
  Colony, Mountains, Coal

Fun Fact: The first peanuts grown in the
  U.S. were grown in Virginia.

Glossary

abolitionists (ab-uh-LISH-uh-nists): people who tried to end slavery

coral reefs (KOR-uhl reefs): rocklike ridges or islands in warm oceans; formed from layers of sea creatures

diverse (di-VURS): different; having a lot of variety

dunes (doons): hills or ridges of wind blown sand

economy (i-KAH-nuh-mee): how a community manages its money and goods for sale

high tide (hye tide): ocean tide when it reaches its highest level

lumber (LUHM-bur): wood sawed into boards for building

peninsula (PUH-nin-suh-luh): land surrounded by water on three sides

plantations (plan-TAY-shuhns): large farms with crops

tourism (TOOR-iz-uhm): traveling for pleasure

tropical (TRAH-pi-kuhl): a region or climate with temperatures high enough to support year-round plant growth given sufficient moisture

Index

Show What You Know

1. How do people dress in the Southern Atlantic region?
2. What is the largest crop grown in Florida?
3. Where did the first battle of the Civil War occur?
4. What is Virginia's motto?
5. What is a peninsula and where is one located in the Southern Atlantic region?

Websites to Visit

www.kidport.com/reflib/usageography/facts/SCarolina.htm

www.factmonster.com/states.html

usa-facts.com/geography

Author

Sue Vander Hook writes geography and history books for children. She grew up on the West Coast in Southern California and lived for five years in south Florida. Her favorite pastime is taking road trips throughout the United States.

Meet The Author!
www.meetREMauthors.com

www.rourkeeducationalmedia.com

PHOTO CREDITS: Title page © FloriaStock; page 3 © fotomark; page 4 © Photomika-com; page 5 © a9photo; page 6 © Bert123; page 7 © bartuchna@yahoo.pl; page 8 © Stephen B. Goodwin; page 9 © Shutterdo; page 10 © Paul Brennan; page 11 © jo Crebbin; page 12 © stephankarkhots; page 13 © A7880S; page 15 Library of Congress; page 16 © 2009 Photolibrary; page 17 © Kali Nine LLC, JacobH; page 18 © Tom Hirtreither; page 19 © Cameron Whitman, natalia Dobryanskays; page 20 © Branislavpudar; page 21 © Jose Antionio Perez; page 22 © max Topchili, D4Fish, artstorm; page 23 © Rhchard Carey; page 24 © msheldrake, Jordan Tan; page 25 © llaszlo, 7436202690; page 26 © Darryl Brooks, NRedmond, page 28-29 © Jenn Huls, Sean Pavone, Achimdiver, Sean Lena, abutyrin, and flags: public domain

Edited by: Jill Sherman

Cover design by: Jen Thomas
Interior design by: Rhea Magaro

Library of Congress PCN Data

Southern Atlantic Coast Region / Sue Vander Hook
(United States Regions)
 ISBN 978-1-62717-676-7 (hard cover)
 ISBN 978-1-62717-798-6 (soft cover)
 ISBN 978-1-62717-915-7 (e-Book)
Library of Congress Control Number: 2014934391

Also Available as:

Printed in the United States of America, North Mankato, Minnesota